MILLICENT E. SELSAM

POPCORN

photographs by Jerome Wexler

William Morrow and Company · New York 1976

Acknowledgments for Photographs

American Museum of Natural History, 10
Corn Refiners of America, 46 left
Field Museum of Natural History, 11
Matthew Lebowitz, 45
Port Authority of New York and New Jersey, 48
United States Department of Agriculture, 7, 38, 44, 46 right, 47 bottom

Library of Congress Cataloging in Publication Data

Selsam, Millicent Ellis, date
   Popcorn.

   SUMMARY: Describes the growth cycle of the type corn used to make popcorn.
   1. Popcorn—Juvenile literature. [1. Popcorn] 1. Wexler, Jerome. 11. Title.
SB191.P64P44   584'.92   76-26627
ISBN 0-688-22083-5
ISBN 0-688-32083-X lib. bdg.

BY THE AUTHOR

Animals as Parents
The Apple and Other Fruits
Bulbs, Corms, and Such
The Carrot and Other Root Vegetables
The Courtship of Animals
The Harlequin Moth
How Animals Live Together
How Animals Tell Time
How to Grow House Plants
The Language of Animals
Maple Tree
Microbes at Work
Peanut
Plants That Heal
The Plants We Eat
Play With Plants
Play With Seeds
Play With Trees
The Tomato and Other Fruit Vegetables
Underwater Zoos
Vegetables From Stems and Leaves

These small, hard corn kernels can *pop* into

6   this tasty white food. So this corn is known as popcorn.

POPCORN SWEET CORN FLOUR CORN FLINT CORN DENT CORN

Other kinds of corn do not pop as well.

Popcorn is a very old type of corn.
In 1964, scientists digging in dry caves
in the Tehuacan Valley of southern Mexico
found small corncobs under an inch long.
They were a type of popcorn
and were over 7,000 years old!

Here is what the tiny cobs looked like.
From the top of the ear,
spikes of male flowers arose.

Scientists don't know for sure
whether the Mexican Indians popped this corn or not.
But possibly cavemen first discovered
that corn could be eaten
when the hard, little seeds of popcorn exploded in a fire
and turned inside out into a tasty food.

Scientists do know that people
who lived in caves in New Mexico 2,000 years ago
did pop corn, because popped kernels of that age
were found there in a cave named Bat Cave.
There were also unpopped kernels in the cave,
and the scientists studying the corn
were able to pop some of these 2,000-year-old kernels.

9

In any case,
popcorn was known to the Indians in America
thousands of years before the arrival of Columbus.
This jug from Peru is about 1,000 years old.
The corncobs modeled on it are related to popcorn.

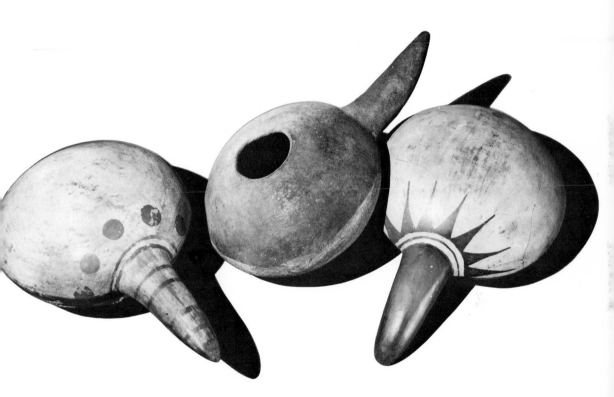

Mexican and South American Indians developed
pottery corn poppers as long as 1,500 years ago.
A shallow vessel, like the ones above,
with a hole on the top and a handle
may have been used to pop corn in.

11

The popcorn plant is small
compared to other corn.
It grows four to six feet tall,
while other corn can grow to twenty feet.

DENT CORN

The usual kind of corn,
grown in the Midwestern United States, is called "dent."
It is seven to ten feet high—
about as high as an elephant's eye.

You can grow popcorn yourself easily.
The popcorn kernels
in the cans you buy in the grocery
can sprout.
Plant about ten seeds at a time,
because only about half of them may germinate
(send out roots and shoots).
Soak the popcorn overnight.
Then look closely at one popcorn grain
before planting it.

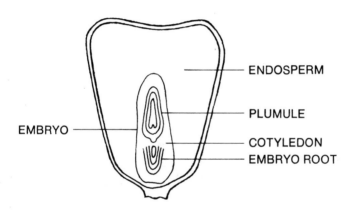

The embryo in the center is the part of the grain
that grows into a new plant.
At the top of the embryo there is an embryo bud
that grows into stem and leaves.
It is called the "plumule."
Opposite it is the embryo root
that will form the root system.

Around the plumule and embryo root
is the seed leaf,
which is called the "cotyledon."
Around the cotyledon
is the part called the "endosperm."
Both the cotyledon and the endosperm
have lots of starch and some protein.
When you plant the seed and water enters,
the food is used by the embryo as it grows.

You can plant the grains directly into soil,
but then you cannot see what happens
until the pale-yellow shoot breaks through the soil.
If you would like to watch
this part of the growth of the popcorn,
plant the grains in a drinking glass
that you can see through.

Line the glass with paper towel.
Stuff it with more paper towel,
and then wet all the paper carefully.
Now place the soaked seed
between the paper and the glass.
Put the glass in a warm place.

15

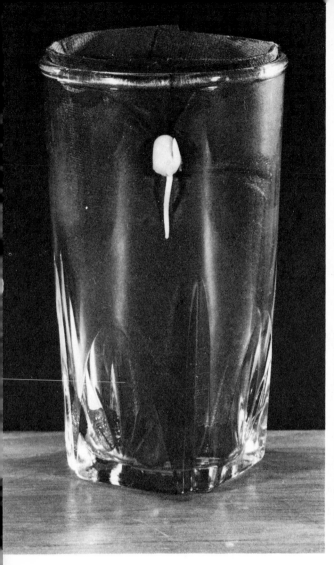

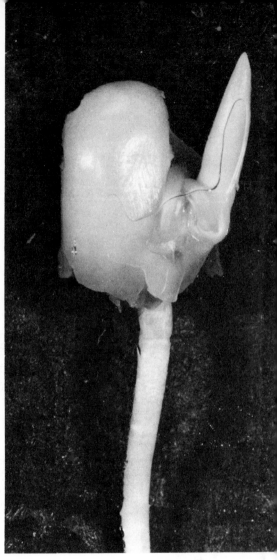

In three to five days,
you will see
a small root emerging.

In another day,
you should see
the plumule growing out
into a sprout
that will become
the stems and leaves.

More roots form.
If you look closely, you can see
tiny little root hairs coming out of the roots.
They are especially clear near the sprout.
The root hairs have very thin walls.
Water can enter easily
and travel through the root hairs into the root.
There it enters special canals
that carry the water to the rest of the plant.

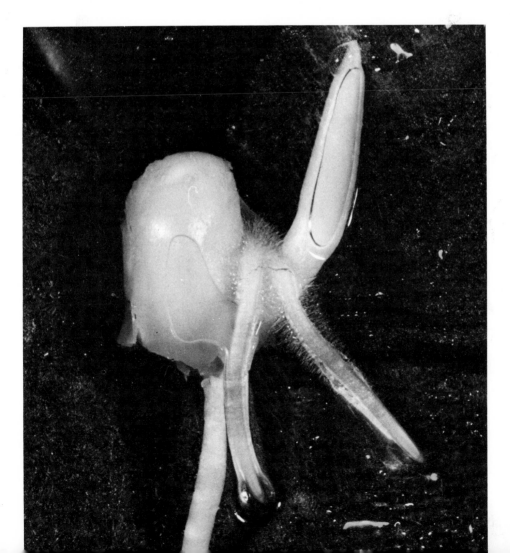

The first leaves form,
and more roots
appear below.
You already have
a tiny popcorn plant.

There is a limit to how big the popcorn plant
can get in a drinking glass.
If you want to find out more
about the growth of the popcorn plant,
you must plant it in soil.

You can plant the popcorn grains in a vegetable garden,
or you can plant them in large ten-inch clay pots
or in plastic garbage cans.
If you use plastic,
you have to punch holes in the bottom.
Use an ice pick or screwdriver.
Get an adult to heat the pick or screwdriver
in a gas flame or on an electric coil of the stove.
Then it will go through the plastic garbage can easily.
Now excess water can drain out of the can.

You can use garden soil
or the potting soil that is sold
in hardware stores, plant stores, or five-and-tens.
Lighten the soil by adding sand or peat moss,
which can be bought in the same places.
A mixture of half potting soil
and half sand or peat moss
makes a good light soil for the popcorn to grow in.

Plant ten seeds in each pot,
and cover with an inch of soil.
When the plants come up,
leave only the strongest one and pull out the rest.
Keep the plant well watered,
and when it is about a foot high,
add liquid fertilizer
(according to directions on the package).

In a few weeks,
you should have a plant that looks like this one.

In another few weeks,
it will reach its full height of about five feet.

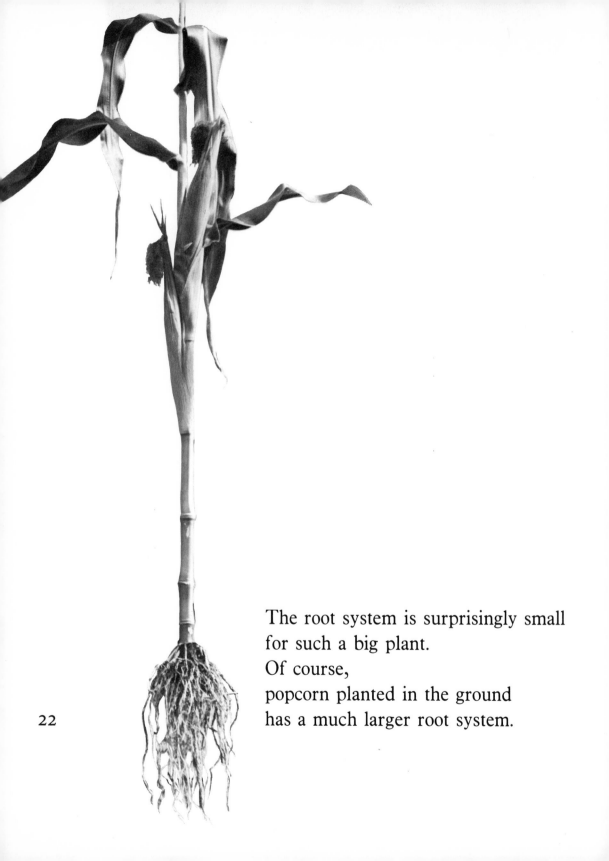

The root system is surprisingly small
for such a big plant.
Of course,
popcorn planted in the ground
has a much larger root system.

At the base of the plant, extra roots grow out.
They help to prop up the tall plant.

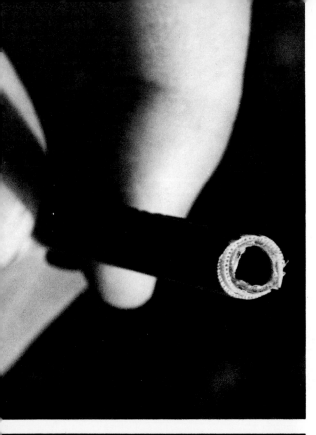

Corn belongs
to the grass family of plants.
Most grasses have stems
with hollow centers.

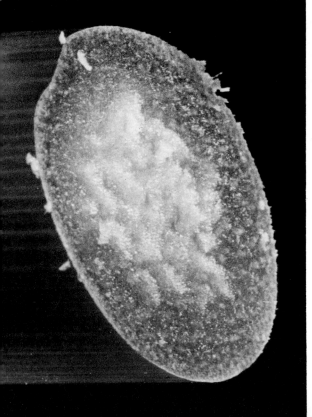

But corn stems are filled
with a soft, spongy tissue,
rich in sugars and starches.
For this reason,
cornstalks are often used
to feed animals.

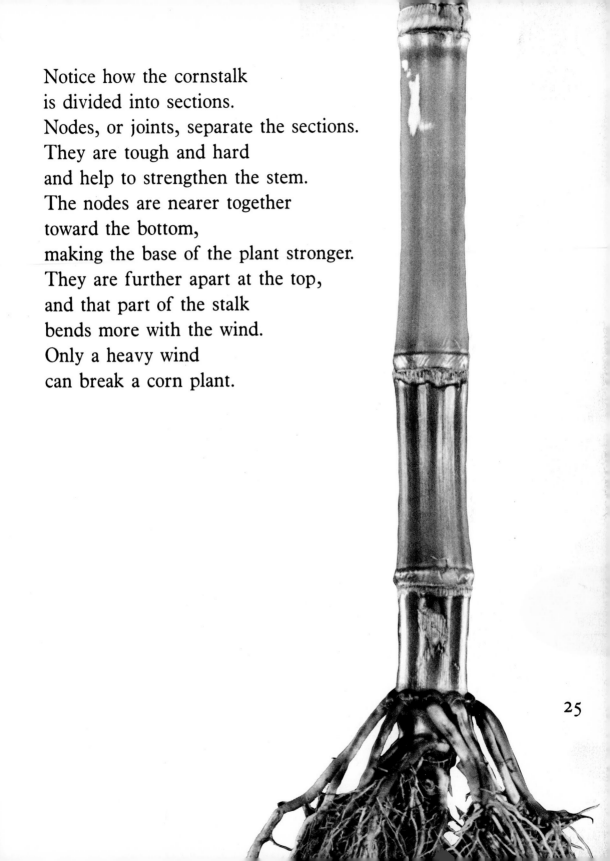

Notice how the cornstalk
is divided into sections.
Nodes, or joints, separate the sections.
They are tough and hard
and help to strengthen the stem.
The nodes are nearer together
toward the bottom,
making the base of the plant stronger.
They are further apart at the top,
and that part of the stalk
bends more with the wind.
Only a heavy wind
can break a corn plant.

25

The leaves are long and emerge at the nodes.
The lower part of the leaf clasps the stem tightly
and helps to strengthen it.

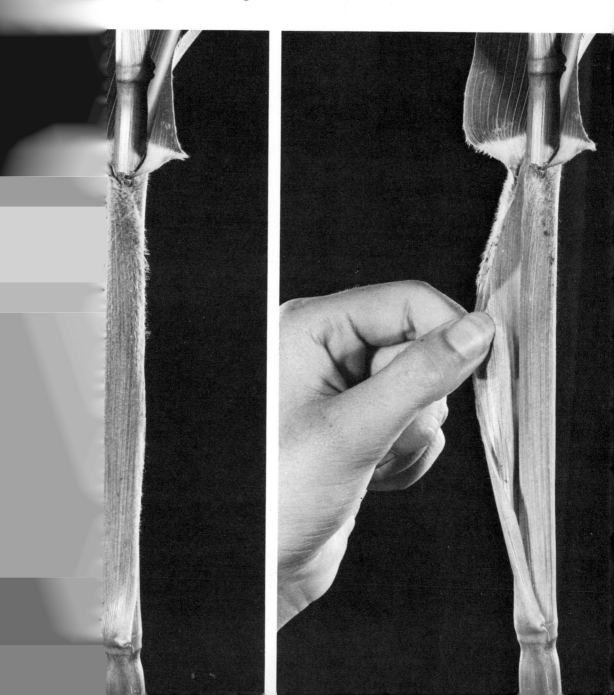

The leaf itself is tough and flexible.
The veins run lengthwise,
and in the center there is a strong central rib.
The edges of the leaf are wavy and do not tear easily.

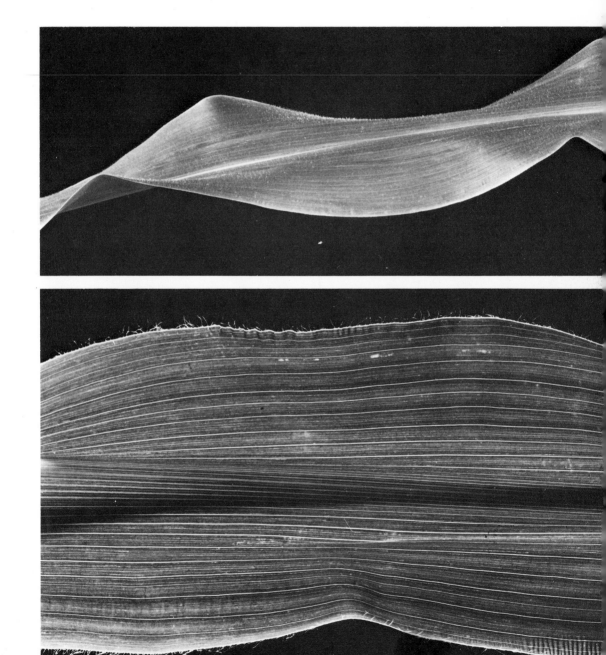

But where does the popcorn come from?
To find out, you have to find the flowers.
Popcorn and all corn plants
have two kinds of flowers: male and female.

The male flowers produce pollen.
They are found in the pale-brown tassels
at the top of the plant.

The female flowers are in the ear,
which forms in the angles of the leaves
on the lower part of the plant.

If you look at a tassel closely,
you can see the individual male flowers.
One flower is open in this picture,
and you can see bags containing pollen hanging down.
They are called "anthers."
When they are in the hanging position,
their pollen is ripe and ready to fall out
when shaken by the wind.
Each corn tassel sheds about ten million pollen grains.
Here the flowers were tapped by hand,
and the pollen started to fall out.

The ear of the corn
is a cluster
of female flowers
sitting on the cob.
If you peel off the husk
(the many layers
of protective leaves
around the cob),
you can find
the individual flowers.
They look like tiny pearls.
The bottom pearllike part
of the flower
is called the "ovary."
Attached to each ovary
is the corn silk.
It extends
as much as five inches
beyond the tip of the ear.

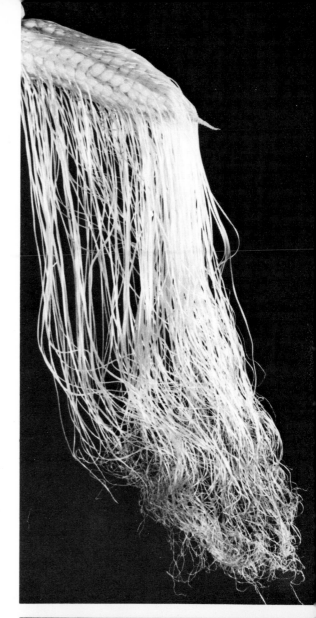

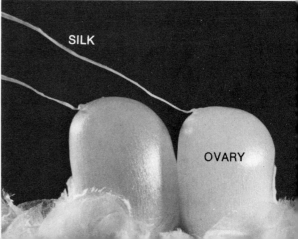

SILK

OVARY

When the silk begins to hang down from the ears,
and each silky strand is covered with fine hairs,

it is ready to receive the pollen.

The wind carries the pollen
to the silky strands hanging out of the ear,
and pollen catches on the fine hairs.
The light pollen grains
can be carried as far as two miles.

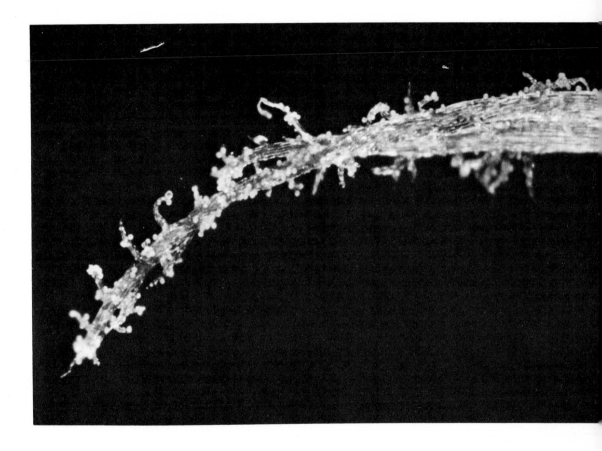

This picture shows the pollen grains
caught on the hairs of the silk.

After a pollen grain lands on a hair,
it grows a pollen tube
down through the center of the long, thin, silky hair,
all the way to the ovary on the cob.
Inside each pollen grain
is a male sex cell called the "sperm nucleus."
Inside each ovary
there is a part called an "ovule."
Inside each ovule
there is a female sex cell, the egg.
When the sperm joins with the egg cell,
the ovule is fertilized and can develop into a seed.
The ovary around the ovule
now develops into the corn kernel.
Technically each corn kernel
is a fruit and not a seed,
because there is an ovary wall
around the developing seed.
Each ovary must receive its own grain of pollen.
If it does not, it does not develop into a kernel.

You can see undeveloped kernels
like the ones in the picture
every time you eat corn.

The ear grows larger
while the ovaries are turning into kernels.
The silky green hairs turn brown.

Here is a popcorn ear
whose kernels are still soft and juicy.
At this early stage, sweet corn is picked.

Popcorn ears, however, are left on the plant
until the kernels mature and dry out.

Thousands of years ago,
popcorn in its wild state could scatter its own kernels.
But it can no longer do so. The kernels stay on the cob.
They stay on the cob of all other types of corn too.
For this reason, farmers have to remove the kernels
from the cobs and plant them.

In the case of popcorn,
the pollen on a plant is released
while the ears on the same plant
are still too young to catch pollen.
Instead, the pollen is blown
to another popcorn plant nearby.
This process is called "cross-pollination,"
and it happens naturally in a field of popcorn.

If you have only one popcorn plant
and want to be sure to get well-developed ears,
you will have to gather your own pollen and keep it
till the ears are ready to receive it.

The anthers of the male flowers
usually emerge in the morning.
Tie a plastic bag around the tassel at this time.
Leave the bag on for several hours.
Shake the tassel before removing the bag.

The pollen is moist and must be dried
before it gets moldy.
To dry, spread the pollen out on newspaper
in a room with little air movement.
After it is dry and powdery, put it in a small jar,
label it, and place it in the refrigerator.

The corn silk is ready to receive pollen
when the silk begins to hang down.
You can check further.
Use a magnifying glass to see
if the hairs are standing out on each strand of silk.
If so, the corn silk is definitely ready.

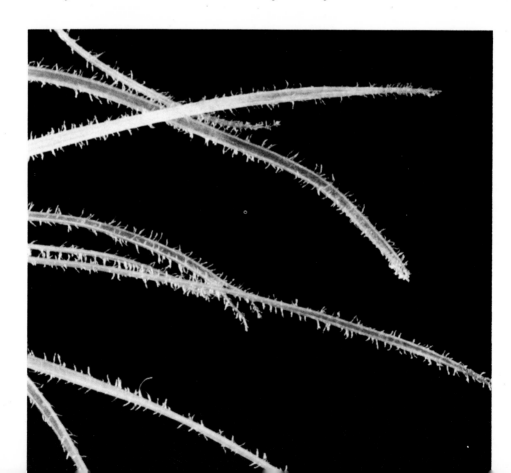

At this time,
dip a small brush into the pollen in the jar
and touch the silk with it.

Now you can watch the ears grow.
The ears have to remain on the plant
till the end of the growing season when they are dry.

Once you husk the corn, dry it further.
Lay the ears on a layer of newspapers.
When they are thoroughly dry,
shell the kernels and store them in jars.
Now you can pop your own popcorn.
Or you can save the corn kernels to plant another crop.
Or you can do both.

Popcorn should begin to pop in one minute,
and one cup of unpopped popcorn should give you
thirty cups of popped popcorn.
The popcorn explodes
when it is heated to 400 degrees Fahrenheit.
The heat changes the moisture inside the kernel to steam.
But the steam cannot escape,
because the kernel has a hard covering.
Finally the pressure inside becomes too much,
the cover breaks,
and the starchy food
inside the kernel
pops out.

Popcorn is only one member
of the large corn family.
Besides popcorn,
you probably are most familiar with sweet corn.
Still, this corn is a relatively small crop.
Most of the six billion bushels of corn
that are grown in this country
are a kind of dent corn,
so called because there is a dent
at the top of each kernel.

Eighty percent of this corn crop
is fed to cattle, pigs, and poultry.
Thus, it helps to produce bacon, pork, beef,
chicken, butter, cheese, and eggs.

The corn kernel contains
about sixty-five percent starch,
nine percent protein, and four percent oil.
In industry, these parts are separated from each other.
The starch and oil are removed from the grain
to be used in many different foods.
The protein that is left over is used to feed livestock.

Over 1,000 items in a supermarket
contain corn oil, cornstarch, or corn sugar.
Cornstarch is easily converted into corn sugar.
Canned fruits and vegetables, jams, jellies, soups,
bread, crackers, cakes, cereals, dessert puddings,
candy, ice cream, soups, sodas, and beer
all contain products derived from corn.

Cornstarch has
many industrial uses.
These cloth fibers
are sized,
or strengthened,
with cornstarch.

The paper on the left
in this picture
was treated with cornstarch.
It is nine times stronger
when wet
than the untreated,
torn paper
shown on the right.

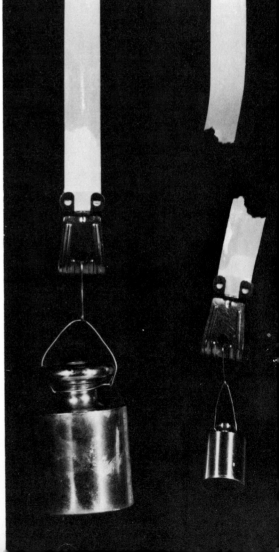

The water in which corn is soaked
is used to grow molds that produce penicillin.

Lightweight foam material like the ones here
are made from the starch of corn.
The foam can be used to insulate the walls of a house.

Does this skyscraper make you think of corn?
Probably not.
But it does contain many products made from corn.

1. Chemicals derived from corn
   slow down the time it takes
   to set the concrete.
2. Cornstarch is used
   in the process
   of making steel from iron ore.
3. Cornstarch plays a role
   in the manufacture
   of plaster wallboards
   and ceiling panels.
4. Products of corn
   are used to manufacture
   asbestos pipe wrap,
   floor tiles,
   fiberglass draperies,
   and many other products
   that go into the inside
   of a skyscraper.

A long history connects
the ancient popcorn
found in caves
to the modern skyscraper.

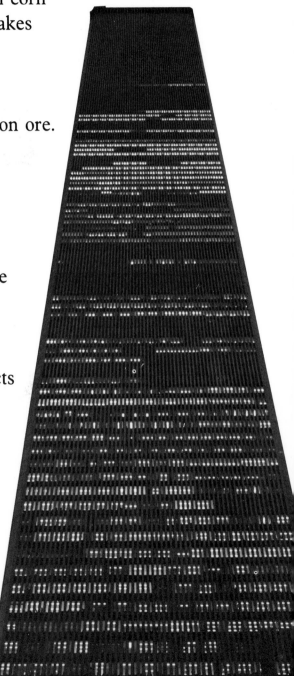